Get Writing!

Write that Film Script

Shaun McCarthy

Heinemann
LIBRARY

www.heinemann.co.uk/library
Visit our website to find out more information about **Heinemann Library** books.

To order:
Phone 44 (0) 1865 888066
Send a fax to 44 (0) 1865 314091
Visit the Heinemann Bookshop at www.heinemann.co.uk/library to browse our catalogue and order online.

First published in Great Britain by Heinemann Library, Halley Court, Jordan Hill, Oxford OX2 8EJ, part of Harcourt Education.
Heinemann is a registered trademark of Harcourt Education Ltd.

Editorial: Lucy Thunder and Helen Cox
Design: David Poole and Susan Clarke
Illustrations: George Hollingworth
Production: Séverine Ribierre
Origination: Dot Gradations
Printed in Hong Kong, China
by Wing King Tong

ISBN 0 431 15211 X
07 06 05 04 03
10 9 8 7 6 5 4 3 2 1

British Library Cataloguing in Publication Data
McCarthy, Shaun
Write that Film Script. – (Get Writing)
808.2′3
A full catalogue record for this book is available from the British Library.

Cover design by David Poole, with illustrations by George Hollingworth

The publishers would like to thank Rachel Vickers for her assistance in the preparation of this book.

Contents

Any words appearing in the text in bold, **like this**, are explained in the glossary.

Making a film

Making a blockbuster film with **special effects** and dozens of actors takes a lot of money. Film **directors** need special and expensive equipment. However, you too can make a film that people will enjoy. All you need is a camcorder, some careful planning and, most importantly, a good **script**.

This book will show you how to turn your ideas into film scripts. All you have to add is your imagination!

Ten minutes

There are all sorts of films, from big action adventures to short stories made for television. In this book, we are going to concentrate on planning and writing the script for a ten-minute drama, a film that tells a made-up story. The ideas in this book can be used for other types of film too, like a **documentary** about things that happen at school.

*A professional film **crew** has highly trained people and special equipment. However, you can make good films using a camcorder, if you have a good script.*

Ten minutes doesn't sound a lot but how much can you fit in?

A lot if you are clever. You can have up to 20 **scenes**, though fewer longer scenes are better. Your script can include versions of all the important things a full-length cinema film has: a gripping story, different **characters**, exciting and interesting speech between actors, changes of **location**. All the things you enjoy in a good film, in fact!

Top tip

Keep things simple! A short story with a small **cast** of characters still needs a lot of work to get right. In a film script, every detail should be worked out before you start filming.

A film script

Here are some things that go into a script. You will learn about these as you work through the book.

- **Dialogue** – everything the actors say to one another.
- Locations – the places where you want to film scenes. You need to know this before you begin filming. Specially made sites for filming are called **sets**.
- Acting **directions** – how and where the actors move. You need to plan this out.
- Camera directions – every movement the camera makes. You need to think about this too – the camera operator needs to know where the actors are going to move!

Activity – film favourites

Think of a film you have really enjoyed. Make a list of up to ten things that you liked about it. Don't just think about the story. The places where it was filmed and the different sorts of characters all add to the pleasure of watching it. Keep this list of things in mind when you plan your film.

All sorts of films

There are as many different varieties of film as there are stories or books. Popular types of film include adventures, mysteries and family stories.

Here is a list of some of the most common kinds of film:

- Horror films
- Comedy films
- Detective films ('cops and robbers')
- Fantasy films
- Science fiction films

Have you seen films that fit into these categories? What were they called? What did they have in common? Can you think of other sorts of film?

You can make your own simple versions of most of these types of films. First though, you need to understand the basic elements that make a particular type of film good. What do films like this usually share? A comedy film is no good if there are no jokes. An action film with no chases, fights or **tension** is boring!

Top tip

It's important to think about what type of film you want to write before you start writing the **script**. Don't start a script as a family comedy, then decide halfway through that you want it to be a serious story about someone running away from home. Viewers will just get confused!

Scary or funny?

Some stories can be told in different ways. For example, they can be serious or funny. A ghost story can be written as a scary film or it can be written to make you laugh (remember the film *Casper*, about a friendly ghost?).

Do not forget that a ghost story still needs certain basic things:

- There must be a mystery and someone who wants to solve it.
- There must be a place where the ghost haunts or the mystery happens.
- There must be **scenes** that build up tension and excitement.
- There must be an ending where things are explained.

Things that make good ghost films:
1. people are told a ghost story
2. they visit a haunted house

Activity – vital ingredients

Look at the list of film types on page 6 again.

- List five things you think all good fantasy films should have.
- Now do the same for comedy films.
- Can you write a very simple story plan for either a fantasy or a comedy film? Include the things you enjoy in films to plan a simple film, one you could perhaps actually make!

The story

The first thing you need to plan is what your film will be about. What story do you want to tell? Make a list of the main events in the story. These will be your main **scenes**. Write just one or two lines about the most important things that will happen in each scene.

Just like any good story, a film needs a beginning, middle and an end. Now see if your film plan can be divided into these three sections.

Top tip

When you have an idea for a story, see if you can describe how it starts in just one sentence. Then write one sentence to describe very simply what happens in the middle, and one more sentence to describe how it ends. These three sentences will give you a clear idea of what your film is going to be about.

Beginnings

Beginnings must get the film going. You must introduce your main **characters**, letting the viewers see whatever is most important about them. This can be done quickly through what they say and do. Imagine a boy walking to school. The bell has gone but he just strolls along. A teacher at the gate tells him to 'Get a move on!', but he just smiles. What does this scene tell us about the character?

Middles

Even a short film may have ten or more scenes in the middle where the story is developed. We need to see different things happening, like some action scenes and some scenes with just **dialogue**. We need to learn more about the main characters: how they react to other characters and how they act in different situations. Don't leave your main character 'off camera' (out of sight) for too long.

Ends

A story should come to a proper ending. It must never look like you just ran out of ideas. *From that day on they were best friends* is a good ending. *They went home to tea* is not so good because it does not say anything really important.

Activity – scene planning

It is not just **drama** films that need a beginning, middle and an end. Imagine you were planning to **shoot** a **documentary** film called 'A day in the life of our school'. You could start early in the morning, filming the caretaker alone in the school, getting it ready for the busy day. Then the film could have lots of scenes showing things that happen during a typical day. The film might end with cleaners tidying the empty classrooms.

Make a list of up to ten scenes for this film. Don't focus only on things that happen in the classrooms. Will there be any out-of-school scenes – for example, teachers or students either at home, on the bus or at the local shop in the evening?

The beginning – the head teacher is often the first to arrive.

The middle – there are all sort of sports played in the gym.

The end – the bell goes at the end of the day.

People and places

How many people do you need in your film to make your story work? Each **character** in a film is important – the **viewers** have to get to know them and to want to know what happens to them as the story unfolds. The actors you need to play the characters in a film are called the **cast**.

Don't have too many characters. There should be one or two who are the most important. For example, in a film about a shy girl going to a new school, you could keep your cast to: the new girl, someone who befriends her, a bully, a 'nice' teacher and maybe a rather scary strict one.

Top tip

Think of ways to cut out minor (less important) characters. Don't have a minor character who only comes into the film to tell people something. Instead, you could have one of the important characters say that they have just met the minor character outside!

Locations

The places where **scenes** are filmed are called **locations**. Think about these when you are planning your film. Fit the location to the subject you are filming so that if you, for example, are making a film about road accidents you could film from a motorway bridge. Get a mix of indoor and outdoor scenes, and perhaps have some in interesting and unusual places – for example, swimming pools or hilltops.

When you are writing the **script**, describe the location in a line at the start of every scene. Sometimes just 'A busy street' or 'Hamid's kitchen' is enough.

Activity – who and where?

Choose one of the two stories below and work out a simple plan for a film using these basic ideas:

- Make a list of the characters you need to tell the story. Start with the most important character, then the next, down to characters who only have small parts in the story. As you need a different actor for each part, you may need to cut some minor characters.
- Make a list of the main locations you would use for the film.

A family go on holiday. There is some sort of mystery where they stay, which they get involved in. The children believe the mystery is real. Their parents think it is silly. But the children solve the mystery with the help of a local person who befriends them.

Two best friends at school have their friendship tested when something happens. They are faced with a difficult decision: one wants to do one thing, the other friend thinks they should do exactly the reverse. A newcomer, a third character, takes the side of one friend against the other. In the end they all become friends.

What the characters say

Everything that the **characters** in a film say to one another is called **dialogue**. You have to get every word right so that the **scenes** feel like real life, with real people talking.

A **script** made up of lots of dialogue is also called a **screenplay**. It is the most creative and imaginative type of film writing. Most screenplays try to make dialogue sound as close to ordinary talking as possible. You might want to set your story back in time and have people talking like 'knights in armour', but remember that this is very difficult. Stories set in the present day are much easier to write because you are writing about the world you know and live in.

Top tip

If characters start talking one way at the start of the film, make sure they still talk that way at the end. A character's way of speaking can change, but only if something happens to change them (for example, a rude person learns to be kinder to others).

Writing dialogue

Here are some handy hints to help you write great dialogue:

- Picture what the characters will be doing while you write the dialogue for the actors to speak. What they say must fit in with what the **viewers** see on the screen. A line of dialogue at the beginning of a scene can tell the viewer where the characters are.
- Think about how a grown up might speak to someone younger, and the other way round.
- Give different characters different ways of talking. A shy person might not finish their sentences; an aggressive person might ask lots of short, sharp questions.

- Think about the mood of each scene. If people are making friends or having fun, they will make funny remarks. If the same people are arguing, they will speak angrily.
- Every word should be there for a reason. If you can't say what the point of a word or line is, then you can **cut** it out.
- Read dialogue out loud before you go off filming. Things that look good on the page can sound awful or be a real tongue-twister to say.

Activity – get talking

Two friends on their way to school find a monkey that has escaped from a circus. They think the monkey will have a nicer life as their pet than performing tricks in the circus. They decide to keep it but have to hide it in the book cupboard in class until the end of school.

Write the dialogue between the friends as they walk along (with the monkey!) towards school. They plan what to do. Make them sound like two different, real people walking along and talking. Use your imagination to bring details into the scene.

Later in the film one of the friends is caught passing bananas into the book cupboard. They have to explain to their strict teacher what they are doing.

Write dialogue for this scene. The way the friends speak in front of the teacher will be different from the earlier scene. Think about how you can make the teacher sound very strict.

Action

Action is everything we see a **character** doing: eating, fighting, hiding. When you are writing a film **script**, always think 'Does the actor really need to say this line? Can it be replaced with an action?' Film is about showing things happen, so 'fewer words, more action' is a good rule. Letting the viewers see characters doing things can make them seem more real.

Camping disaster

Imagine a comic **scene** showing two people camping. They have never put up a tent before and make a complete mess of it. You don't need any **dialogue**; they don't need to say 'Oh, this is too hard!' Just use film to show them struggling with ropes and poles, and falling over the flapping tent.

Top tip

For some action, you need things for characters to use. These are called **props**. Always list the props you will need before you start filming a scene. For example, in a scene with pirates looking at a treasure map, you need a map. Maybe one of the pirates has some gold coins which he says are like the ones in the buried treasure.

Action not words

Imagine a dramatic scene in a mystery film where two people think they are being followed along the street. One says to the other 'I think we're being followed.' The other says 'Oh no, I'm scared. Let's run!'

This scene would be better without any dialogue. Have the two people walking, looking behind them nervously. Then **cut to** someone behind them. They speed up; so does the follower. Without using words, it is clear to the **viewer** that the two are being followed.

You can write actions in a film script like this:
(The kitchen. Morning.) Andie is tearing wrapping paper from her birthday present. Cut to ***close-up*** *of brother smiling. Close-up of Andie's face. She finishes unwrapping. Her smile fades. It is not the present she wanted.*

Activity – speaking without words

Imagine this scene. Mum has cooked tea for Jenny, her daughter. Jenny promised to be home at six but comes in at seven, and is worried about what will happen. Mum is cross, but gets the tea from the oven. Her step-dad is also angry but is reading a paper. No one speaks.

Write notes describing how you might **shoot** this scene. How could Jenny, mum and her step-dad show how they are feeling without speaking. For example, Jenny will sit down carefully and quietly and smile at mum. Mum will slam the oven door. What might her step-dad do?

To help you plan this scene, think about looks on people's faces, glances that people give each other, the way they move and stand, the way they handle things. These can all show us how they are feeling.

What goes into a script?

When you look at a film **script** it can be quite hard to read. You might find only a couple of lines of **dialogue** on a page. The rest is descriptions of the **set** or **location**, of the things that are happening and how they are recorded by the camera. A well-written script should paint a clear picture of everything happening on screen. It is quite hard to do!

Key things in a script

A film script is made up of:

1 introductions saying where each **scene** happens
2 all the lines the actors speak, sometimes with basic descriptions of how they speak
3 descriptions of actions that take place
4 instructions to the camera operator about how best to film the scene (for example, saying if the camera will move or go close in to someone's face).

The sample script on page 17 is a simple scene. **Character** names are in capitals. **Directions** for how lines are said are in *italics* and brackets. The notes in each margin tell you what everything means.

Activity – action!

Two friends go camping. One gets up early and cooks over an open fire. After doing a few things he calls his friend. Breakfast is ready! The friend in the tent crawls out. She doesn't like camping. The cook hands her some of what he has made. The grumpy friend looks in horror at the food and is rude about it.

Write a page of script for this scene like the one shown on page 17. Write lines for the actors to say and describe important actions you want the actors to make.

Introduces where the scene is set ('Exterior' means outside)

(Exterior, early morning)

Camera shows a quiet street, all the windows of the houses are still curtained. There is a milk float parked in the distance.

Describes what we see

Describes the actor's actions

Tom is pushing bike out of the garden gate. He yawns. He hoists a newspaper delivery bag on to his shoulder. He looks bored and fed up. He gets on his bike and pedals off slowly.

Camera moves beside Tom as he cycles along. He passes the milkman.

Describes the camera shot and what Tom is doing

The milkman's line, with a note about how it is said

MILKMAN: *(Brightly)* Morning Tom, lovely morning!

TOM: *(Fed up)* Yeah, great.

Tom's line, with a note about how it is said

MILKMAN: You should get to bed earlier!

Describes how the scene ends and leads us to the cut into the next shot

The milkman walks off whistling. Tom, half asleep, wobbles on his bike. Cut to ...

(Interior, paper shop. Tom enters.)

Introduces the next scene ('Interior' means indoors)

Planning with pictures

A professional film **script** is always read along with a **storyboard**. A storyboard is like a strip cartoon. It is a series of simple pictures in boxes showing key events in the film in the right order. It helps you plan how the film will look.

You need to make a storyboard to go with your script. You don't have to be a brilliant artist; stick people are fine!

Storyboard pictures

The storyboard pictures help you plan **camera angles** and the positions of actors and **props** when you start to **shoot** each **scene**. For a ten-minute film you will probably need ten little pictures for a really good storyboard, or less if you are only having a few key scenes. Each picture must show roughly how you think the scene should be shot, for example **close-up** on the actors, or from further away so that they are seen against a background.

Activity – stick people go camping

Make a ten-picture storyboard for the following story. Keep the pictures simple and give each one a short caption.

Two friends go camping. (It could be our friends from the last page.) They pitch their tent in a field under a mountain. In the night, they are frightened by an owl, then by sheep. In the morning, one friend cooks breakfast over a smoking fire. They spend their first day climbing a mountain. It rains and the wind blows. That night it is still raining and the tent blows down. A bull comes into the field so they escape up a tree. The farmer comes out and rescues them in his Land Rover. They spend the night in his nice warm barn.

Storyboard captions

Each picture in a storyboard has a line saying what it is about. This is called a caption. The best way of creating a caption is to use a line from the script. This can be something one of the actors says, or a description of an important happening.

In a film where someone discovers a beautiful old car in an abandoned garage, you would have a picture of this scene like the one below. Someone is pushing open the door. Sunlight falls onto the dusty but lovely old car. You can caption this scene with a line of **dialogue**, like '*Tom, look at what I've found!*' Or you could have a description of what is happening: *Adam pushes open the door and gazes in*. The camera **direction** could be: '*zoom in slowly towards the car through garage door*.'

Top tip

Making a film is difficult, even with simple equipment. Planning what you want to do is very important. Having the script and the storyboard all worked out before you go out and shoot the first scene will make things much easier.

Characters and real people

In a **drama**, you make up **characters** to be played by people acting. In a **documentary** film, you use real people who appear in the film as themselves. You should never mix made-up characters with real people in the same film. In your film, people should either play parts you have written for them in a drama, or be themselves in a documentary.

Let's look at how to develop characters in **script** writing.

Actors and characters

In a drama, the **director** will discuss with the actors how to bring their characters to life. Actors think about how characters might walk, sit, move and react to events. They invent details to make their characters interesting.

Know your characters

When planning a drama film, make some notes about each character. Who are they? What is their part in the film? How do they get on with other characters? Try to think of them as real people and use your imagination to make notes about their habits, interests, ways of talking and so on. Make sure that they are different from each other.

Top tip

Some actors find it really does help to put yourself in somebody else's shoes. So if you – or an actor in your film – are stuck with a character and they don't seem real, imagine what they have on their feet. You really do feel different in high heels than trainers!

Real people

You get an interesting **cast** in a documentary by having a wide a range of different people involved. In the 'Day in the life of our school' film, you want teachers, parents and caretakers as well as a wide range of students to take part. You don't write lines of **dialogue** for them, you get them to speak 'as themselves'. Remember, even in a documentary you should try to concentrate on two or three main figures to follow through the film.

Activity – thinking in character

Imagine two people who are best friends, even though they are very different people. Then one of them does something (not to the other one) that challenges their friendship. What could it be? Perhaps they are faced with a difficult and important decision in their life and they do something that their friend just can't understand. After all sorts of problems, things are sorted out. The two best friends become even closer.

Develop your characters. Using your imagination, make notes describing them. Give them names. How are they different? Why are they friends? What things do they do together? What are they like with other people when they are on their own? How do they behave towards other people when they are together? Try to invent as much detail as you can about each of your imaginary characters.

Marsha and Reena are best friends although they are very different. Marsha is loud, always the centre of attention. Reena is quieter …

Combining words and action

Your **script** must include both words and actions. How do you make them work together to bring your **scene** to life?

Think of the details

A scene can be several people talking round a table. Or it can be someone walking down a street and buying an apple. When you are writing your script, you need to ask yourself 'What do I want **viewers** to understand in this scene?' Every scene must have one most important point and you need to know exactly what it is as you write.

Decisions, decisions!

Start with the beginning of each scene. What's the first thing we see? Will the main **character** open the door and walk into a room to meet someone? Or will we start with two people together in the room? We could have a little scene showing one character making his or her way towards the room, or even outside in the road heading towards the building.

All these choices and we haven't even got to the first line of **dialogue**!

Top tip

You can work out how to film your scenes by thinking of all possible options, then deciding which might work best. If you can't decide, try ***shooting*** *different versions, then pick the way that seems to work best. You don't always have to stick to the idea you wrote in the script. Remember to plan well though, before you start shooting.*

The right length

As the scene develops, make sure the dialogue and the actions stick to the main point of the scene. You will soon get a sense of when a scene is the right length – you will know when to end it before it becomes dull.

Activity – putting it together

Kara is behind with her homework. She has promised her mum that her best friend Seema is coming round to help her with it. In fact, they stay in Kara's room all evening, playing computer games, eating sweets and reading magazines. Suddenly, Mum bursts into Kara's room. She is suspicious. Kara tries to convince her mum that they have been working. Seema is a bit stuck. She doesn't want Kara's mum to think she is responsible for what has been happening.

Try writing this scene, starting with Kara and Seema having fun before Mum comes in. What happens next? What does everyone say? Think of things that can happen in the bedroom, like Kara trying to slide magazines and sweet wrappers under the bed without Mum seeing. Describe some actions. How does the scene end?

Filming real life

Let's look at two types of writing you need for **documentary** films, which are films about events that happen in real life.

Asking questions

Questions are used in documentary films where you **interview** real people. They are very important; they affect the whole purpose of your film.

Think about what the main point in each **scene** is – what do you want to interview people about? Plan your questions carefully so you get interesting answers from the people you interview. You might not use them all, especially if the person being interviewed has a lot to say.

Top tip

Don't ask questions in interviews that can be answered with just 'yes' or 'no'. Instead of saying 'Were you happy when you won the game?' ask 'How exactly did you feel when you won?' Ask questions that encourage people to give details.

Commentary

In some documentary films you hear the voice of someone who describes something taking place on screen, but who is not seen on camera (for example, as in wildlife programmes). This voice is called a commentary, or 'voice over'. It must be carefully written out, read at the right pace and added to the right parts of the scene so that everything fits together. The good thing about the commentary is that you control exactly what is said.

Imagine a person doing some unusual job. The camera records what they are doing. They might explain things while they work (like a sort of interview) or you might write your own commentary (description) and record it over the scene afterwards.

A commentary for a gardening programme might go like this: *'Here is Jake planting a triffid, the rare man-eating plant. He is doing this because he hates Jeremy, the other presenter, and hopes the triffid will get him later on … Now he's finished planting … Nice work Jake … Watch out Jeremy!'*

Activity – doing a voiceover

Record a scene from television that you think you could write a commentary for. Gardening, cooking or DIY programmes are good for this. You only need a short scene that lasts two or three minutes.

Run the scene with the sound off. Time it.

Now write your own commentary to go over the scene. It needs to last for the same time as the scene will take to be shown. It should describe exactly what is happening on the screen, but you can add your own ideas.

Run the scene and read your commentary out loud. **Cut** it or make it longer if necessary so that it fits the scene.

Using the camera

Even a film **shot** with one camcorder needs to have some camera **directions** included in the **script**. The camera operator needs a clear idea of what they must do in each **scene**. You need to include some basic directions.

Camera directions

Here are some types of camera shot and what they mean.

- **Establishing shot** – a shot at the start of a scene that tells **viewers** where the film is happening. This is essential so that viewers do not get lost straight away. The camera might be high up and the shot moves across a city, then down to the street where a **character** is walking along. This 'establishes' or lets us know that we are in a big city.

- Panning shot – the camera swings round to show the scene around it.
- **Tracking** shot – the camera follows someone walking, or running, for example. Or it moves past something standing still, like the view you'd get from a moving car.
- **Cut to** – the screen goes black for a moment. Then the next thing we see is a different scene. It creates a break.
- **Close-up** – filming a person's face or an object very close to, so that it fills the whole screen.

Planning directions

When planning camera directions, ask yourself questions like: if two people are talking, do you cut to each of them separately in close-up when they speak? Or do you show them both together in one long shot? Showing them together is usually best. You don't have to keep changing the shot.

Think about using interesting **camera angles**. If someone is hiding up a tree, filming them from underneath the tree makes them look much higher up and makes the shot more exciting.

Activity – classroom drama

Imagine you had to shoot this scene:

A group of pupils are waiting outside a classroom for the teacher to come and let them in. They push, shove and chatter. Then they see the teacher coming round a corner of the corridor. Everyone goes quiet and gets into a proper line. The teacher watches them carefully, then opens the door. They rush to their places. Suddenly, they notice a Roman soldier standing in the corner – this is going to be a different sort of history lesson!

Don't write any **dialogue**; just make a list of possible shots you could use to film this scene. Here are some examples:

1. The corridor. The camera tracks beside a ragged line of pupils mucking about as they wait to go into class.

2. Close-up on door. The name on the door is 'Ms Jepson'.

3. Ms Jepson, a very strict teacher, suddenly comes round a corner at the top of the corridor.

4. Close-up on her face – very fierce-looking!

It's a wrap!

'It's a wrap!' is the last thing a **director shooting** a film says. It means 'we've finished!' This guide is about **script** writing rather than actually shooting the film, so you have to 'wrap' when you decide the script is finished.

Read your finished script through carefully. Use the checklists below to make sure you have included everything. Don't forget to check your spelling, punctuation and grammar too!

The story

- Does the story have a proper beginning, middle and end?
- Does the beginning start things in a way that will keep people interested?
- Does the middle have a mix of different types of **scenes**; for example, people talking, action, things happening indoors, then outdoors?
- Does the end of the script wrap the story up in a satisfying way?

Characters and dialogue

- Have you made a cast of interesting, different people?
- Do **characters** sound like separate, individual people? Try to imagine them as real people.
- If a character has a certain way of talking to start with, do they keep it? The way a character talks shouldn't change as the film goes on.
- Are there places where the **dialogue** isn't necessary? Every line should be there for a reason.

Action

- Have you written clear descriptions of the important things that actors will do?
- Are there places where actions could replace words?

How the film will look

- Have you made a **storyboard** to create pictures of important scenes?
- Do your camera **directions** give a plan of how each scene might be filmed?
- Have you started each new scene with an **establishing shot** or a line of dialogue to let the viewer know where they are?
- Have you thought of any interesting ways to use the camera, for example, filming a shot from an unusual position, from low down or high up?

@

Activity – the crew

If you can, put together a '**crew**' of actors, camera person and director and shoot your film!

If you can't shoot a film, try acting out the key scenes. You will be the director. You tell people what to do in each scene. Try to imagine it on screen. Do you think it works? Does the script contain the right lines for the actors? If not, make changes.

Glossary

camera angle direction in which the camera is taking the picture, for example, from above looking down

cast all the actors in a film

character part or role played by an actor

close-up camera shot making a person or object fill the screen. A close-up is often used so we can see the expression on someone's face or see them doing something with their hands.

crew everyone, apart from the actors, who works on making the film – for example, all the people who work the cameras and lights

cut remove unwanted words or parts of a film

cut to camera shot where you stop filming, then start again immediately on the same scene a moment later, but from a different position or angle

dialogue speech between two or more actors

directions instructions, usually given by the director, on how actors should work or how cameras should operate

director the person in charge of making the film. They organize the shooting of every scene. They and the scriptwriter are the people who have most control over what the finished film will be like.

documentary factual film in which real people appear as themselves

drama story involving characters to be played by actors

edit when you finish writing a story you edit it by reading through and making changes. When you make a film you edit by cutting out bad bits and shooting new scenes to go in their place.

establishing shot shot at the start of a scene that shows us where it is taking place. Often the camera shows the wide view then comes down to the characters doing something.

interview to ask someone questions about a chosen topic

locations places where you will shoot your film

props any objects that are needed in a film

scene place where the action takes place

screenplay detailed script of a film that includes technical information like camera direction

script copy of a text of a play used by an actor or director for rehearsing with

sets specially constructed or put together places, usually interiors or rooms, where you shoot scenes of a film

shoot filming with a camera

slang informal language, used instead of formal, 'correct' language; for example 'cool'

special effects tricks used in cinema films to make impossible things happen on screen, such as people running through walls

storyboard series of sketches, like a strip cartoon, showing the major scenes in a film

tension nervous excitement that comes from waiting for events in a film or book to happen

tracks or **tracking** camera direction where the camera moves along, often used to follow actors moving

viewer person watching a film

Find out more

The following books will help you learn more about films. Try reading them and get writing for yourself!

20th Century Media: 1990s, Electronic Media, Steve Parker (Heinemann Library, 2002). This book gives information about films and what technology is used now.

Eyewitness: Film, Richard Platt (Dorling Kindersley, 2000). More information about films.

Index

Titles in the *Get Writing* series include:

Hardback 0 431 15211 X

Hardback 0 431 15215 2

Hardback 0 431 15210 1

Hardback 0 431 15212 8

Hardback 0 431 15213 6

Hardback 0 431 15214 4

Find out about the other titles in this series on our website www.heinemann.co.uk/library